Writing Up Cutting Up:

Anthropoetry at The Edge of The Human

Edited by Maxime Le Calvé
With a foreword by Stuart McLean

Anthro)Re(Verb

This work is licensed under the Creative Commons Attribution 4.0 Licence (BY), which permits the editing, reproduction and distribution of the material in any format or medium for any purpose, including commercial use, provided the author is credited.
https://creativecommons.org/licenses/by/4.0/
The terms of the Creative Commons licence apply only to original material. The reuse of material from other sources (labelled with the source) such as diagrams, illustrations, photos and text excerpts may require further usage permissions from the respective rights holder.
Published in 2024 by AnthroReverb, Berlin.
Cover design: Mudar Al-Khufash
Cover illustration: picture by Tsz Man Chan at Papay Gyro Nights, used with permission (cut out © Maxime Le Calvé)
Design: Mudar Al-Khufash
Typesetting: Mudar Al-Khufash
The author gratefully acknowledges the support of the Cluster of Excellence "Matters of Activity. Image Space Material", funded by the German Research Foundation (DFG) as part of the Excellence Strategy of the German Federal and State Governments - EXC 2025 - 390648296.
DOI: doi.org/10.21428/80e887d9.9547e9a3
ISBN 978-3-9826419-2-8

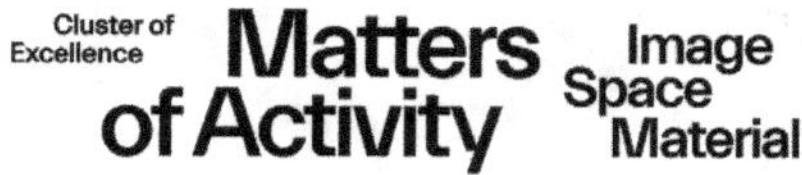
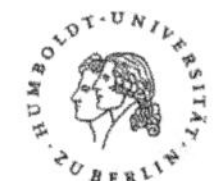

Table of Contents

Foreword
Other Anthropoetries?
Stuart McLean

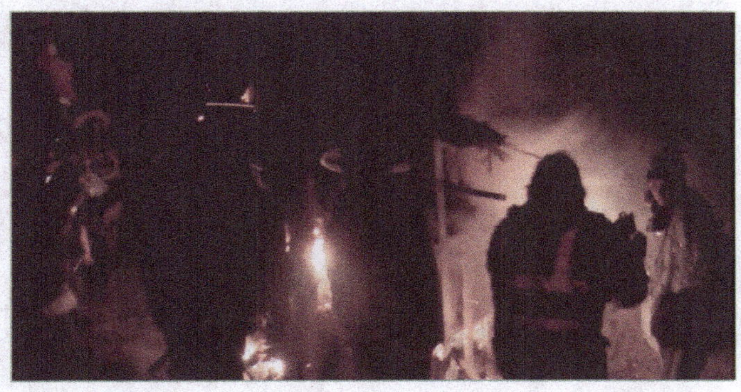

Reading these contributions, I feel honored that my workshop provided the occasion for these fine and various pieces of writing. Anthropology remains contemporary as long as its practitioners are prepared to keep reinventing it. So here are a few scattered thoughts about poetry.

poetry comes in many shapes and sizes
including, sometimes, the shape of prose[1]
or prose can be disassembled, reassembled
in the shape of verse
poetry is a refusal
of containment
and an affirmation
of being uncontained

poetry opens borders
when most of us hear the word "poetry"
we are inclined perhaps
to think of lyric poetry
which is most of the poetry
written today

short, often first person
gaze turned inward
on thoughts and feelings
that are often denied a place
in academic prose

not surprising then
that many fine experiments in "anthropoetry"
have followed just such a course

Adrie Kusserow's explorations in verse
of the traumatized subjectivities
of Sudanese lost boys and girls
detained in the limbo of refugee camps
or struggling to make new lives
in the suburban United States[2]

Renato Rosaldo's antropoesía
through which he revisits
decades after the event
the death of his partner, anthropologist Shelly Rosaldo
who missed her footing and fell
from a cliff on the island of Luzon

[1]   See   for   example   Adrie   Kusserow's   recent   The   Trauma   Mantras:
A   Memoir   in   Prose   Poems.   Durham: Duke   University   Press,   2024.
[2]   Adrie   Kurrerow,   "Anthropoetry."   In   Anand   Pandian   and   Stuart   McLean   ed.   Crumpled   Paper
Boat: Experiments   in   Ethnographic   Writing.   Durham: Duke   University   Press,   2017,   71-90.

in the Philippines[3]

for both of these anthropologist-poets
lyric provides a conduit
for all that scholarly writing
in its more conventional forms
seeks to exclude

anger, desire, grief, pain, remorse, self-doubt . . .

all the mess that muddies claims to expertise
and that moody Malinowski sought to siphon off
into the safe container of his strict-sense-of-the-term diary
only to have it leak out – all too messily - in posthumous
publication[4]

still, feelings are not the only kind of mess
and lyric is not the only kind of poetry

for the ancient Greeks
lyric poetry was so-called
because it was sung
to the accompaniment
of a lyre[5]

a techno-prosthesis of sorts
plucked sounds amplifying and extending
human language
or channeling the vibrations

[3]   Renato Rosaldo, The Day of Shelly's Death. Durham: Duke University Press, 2014.
[4] Bronislaw Malinowski, A Diary in the Strict sense of the Term. Stanford: Stanford University Press, 1989.
[5] Cecil Bowra, Greek Lyric Poetry: From Alcman to Simonides. Oxford: Oxford University Press, 1961, 3.

of a world before words

but lyric was just one kind of poetry among others

there was also dramatic poetry
spoken in the course
of a theatrical performance
individually voiced characters
late arrivals on the scene
preceded by the Chorus
a voice of collective enunciation
prior to the splitting of selves

might the Chorus too hearken back
to a place beyond the human?

more ancient than lyric or dramatic poetry
more ancient than writing
is epic poetry

before Aeschylus, Sophocles, Euripides
was the artist subsequently known as Homer
recounter of the travails
of gods and heroes
and of Odysseus's
long journey home[6]

and before Homer
Hesiod
bard of theogony

[6] Homer, The Odyssey. Translated by. Walter Shewring. Oxford: Oxford University Press, 1998.

the coming-to being
of gods and universe
battling primordial forces
extravagantly bodied Titans
the neatly proportioned Olympian gods
a late-in-the-day victory
over a turbulent all-that-came-before[7]

or tracking backward and eastward
to once-was-Mesopotamia
and the cosmogonic clash
of Marduk and Tiamat
victory for him
her vanquished, precursor body
dismembered and repurposed
as architecture
of a new universe[8]

or centuries later
Lucretius
physicist-poet
likening his own verses
to the cascading, colliding atoms
that make and unmake
everything and everyone
himself included[9]

epic speaks
of and from a time and space
before the lyric "I"

[7] Hesiod, Theogony/ Works and Days. Translated by M. L. West. Oxford: Oxford University Press, 1988.
[8] Stephanie Daley, ed. And trans., Myths from Mesopotamia. Oxford: Oxford University Press, 1989.
[9] Lucretius, On the Nature of the Universe. Translated by R. E. Latham. London: Penguin, 2005.

speaks of ontogenesis
of cosmogenesis
of the coming-to being
of worlds
not only human

is it over now, like Tiamat and the Titans?
a victim of the usual suspects
capitalism
Western hegemony
the Disenchantment of the World
the Great Divide of "Nature" from "Culture"?

in place of epic expansiveness
Modernity's Great Indoors
home to a polite plurality
of similarly unique individuals
gods and nature spirits whittled down
to psychic projections
chthonic and elemental powers
displaced by me-feelings

has epic gone?
or made way for epigone?

like the diluted nationalist variants
spawned in Romanticism's wake
national epics shrinking polyphony
to a single, mobilizing voice
demarcating belonging from not

with lines ever more sharply etched[10]

is national epic the lyric
of the ethno-subject
as securitized, single-celled self
writ large and shouted loud?

Brexit poetry
MAGA poetry
 poetry so bad
it becomes anti-poetry
anti-becoming
anti-worlding
the not-poetry
of the not-open-to-question
we know who we are
and it's not you

but epic is the poetry
of what is before
or between
or around
"You" and "I"

the poetry of what makes "Us"
any "Us"
possible

not a readymade form
to be used or discarded

---

[10] On intersections between epic poetry, nationalism, and imperialism, see Colin Graham, Ideologies of Epic: Nation, Empire, and Victorian Epic Poetry.　Manchester: Manchester University Press, 1998.

or assigned its place
on a straight, white, European timeline
but a tendency that perdures
even in the poetry
we think of as lyric

British poet Alice Oswald writes:

Sometimes epic is no more than a whiff of darkness, a shiver of not knowing that passes under the surface of a poem, but if you miss its movement then you're left with only small, personal, sealed up poetry, the poetry of what has been, rather than what might be.[11]

epic is the universe pressing into words
which can happen wherever
whenever

poetry leans toward epic when it becomes
a jailbreak from solipsism
an expeditionary foray
into worlding substance
vaster than any conceivable "I"Chapter

[11]   Alice   Oswald,   "Lines."   (https://podcasts.ox.ac.uk/lines-alice-oswald).

Cutting Up
/an Introduction
Maxime Le Calvé

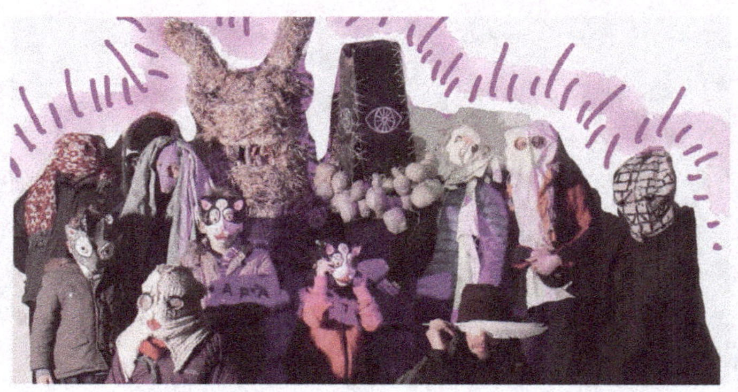

@ picture by Tsz Man Chan at Papay Gyro Nights , used with permission (cut out @ Maxime Le Calvé)

"What new possibilities for thinking and living might result from extending the notion of creativity beyond the human realm?"
— Stuart McLean

This edited collection is the fruit of a day-long writing workshop, invited by the practice and prompts of Stuart McLean. I hosted this workshop part of the stretching senses school, a collective of anthropologists, artists, coders and designers that ran for a while after the stretching materialities exhibition at the Excellence Cluster "Matters of Activity" at Humboldt University in Berlin. [1] The spacious "central laboratory" of the cluster, with its high windows and whitewashed picknick tables, was welcoming yet another interdisciplinary experiment. This time, we looked and sensed the inherent activities of fieldwork materials, as revealed by writing up and cutting up verses from them.

We engaged with the exercises at the end of the workshop. While the session was relatively short, we felt supercharged by the framework planted by Stuart. It would be reducing to say that a simple exposure to his approach sufficed; certainly some of it felt like mere energy transfer. After a thorough lecture introducing us to his views of the power of poetry in the light of an anthropology "at the edge of the human", and to his field work in the British Isles, and a delightful lunch which must also be mentioned, we watched two uncut video sequences extracted from his material. Raw fragments. Indelible fieldwork impressions. The footage was drawn from his involvement in Papay Gyro Nights, a festival of experimental and multimedia arts held annually on the island of Papa Westray in Orkney, Scotland. As Stuart announced before by way of the blurb of the workshop: "The festival draws its name and inspiration from a giantess commemorated in North Atlantic storytelling and performance traditions, who is herself a hybrid figure combining a range of conventionally male and female, human and animal, marine and terrestrial attributes." And what we could see from the videos was nothing short of that. Following Stuart's impulse, we attended to the video material as a means to harness a different relation to the more-than-human entities that we could sense, sieving from the visual notes.

The prompts of Stuart are beautifully expounded and reflected on in the foreword to this collection: We tried to write on an "epic" mode, as opposed to a "lyrical" one, as a way to relate to presences we perceived through the fieldwork material rather than to express our own subjective feelings. During the first segment of the writing session, we produced short accounts in prose. We wrote what we have seen in two video fragments.[2] We wrote what we felt in it. Some of us wrote by hand, others typed it straight up on their laptops. After that, Stuart invited us to use "free verse" to invite the presences and spirits to our table: slashing our prose to pieces and bringing into it our bodily respirations, the words radiated with new auratic qualities. Reading them aloud in a final round was a brave, an emotional act for some of us, as the writing process and cut-up it induced brought into the room a wealth of other presences from our own, which lent substance and energy to those brought by Stuart. It felt as a gift to Stuart and to these beings that he pays respect to through the fieldwork, the living, the dead, and the spirits around the table; this wasn't exempt of eery sensations, and yet, it was a moment full of warmth as we were giving each other access to personal haunted bouts of drafting and cutting, of whatever happened on the page.

[3] David Abram, The Spell of the Sensuous: Perception and Language in a More-than-Human World (New York: Vintage Books, 1997).

We were experiencing first-hand the redistribution of creativity to the multitude, something that Stuart announced in the invitation:

> "The worlds that humans often pride themselves on creating are not and have never been exclusively human but are dependent upon and inflected by a multitude of other-than-human powers and presences, including animals, plants, geological formations, weather systems, and a range of humanly manufactured artifacts fashioned from a variety of materials." (from the abstract of the workshop)

During the preambule lecture, along with the usual roster of writers we have learned to recognize as the sacred citation cluster when discussing the more than human in anthropology (Donna Haraway, Vinciane Despret, Isabelle Stengers, Anna Tsing, Karen Barad, Marisol de la Cadena, Philippe Descola, Emanuele Coccia, Eduardo Kohn, and Michel Serres), Stuart McLean came with an unusual and energetic reference. In the domain of poetic writing, Alice Oswald's practice has shined a new light on how writing can unfold into profound engagement with the more-than-human – reminiscent to some extent to the propositions of the philosopher David Abram in his seminal work *The Spell of The Sensuous*[3] Drawing from the realm of nature, Oswald intricately weaves the nonhuman into her verses, offering it not just a space but a voice that reverberates with its own vitality.[4] Her poems frequently collapse the boundaries between the human and the nonhuman, with an emphasis on rhythm, sound, and the kinetic energy of the natural world. Here from the final page of her book Dart, in which she investigates the soul of a river in Cornwall after doing her own kind of fieldwork:

[4] Alice Oswald, The Thing in the Gap-Stone Stile, 1. publ. in Oxford poets, reissued in new format, Oxford Poets (Oxford: Oxford Univ. Press, 1997); Alice Oswald, Dart (London: Faber and Faber, 2002); Alice Oswald, Woods Etc (London: Faber and Faber, 2005); Alice Oswald, Weeds and Wild Flowers (London: Faber and Faber, 2009).

> "With their grandmother mouths, with their dog-soft eyes, asking who's this moving in the dark? Me. This is me, anonymous, water's soliloquy, all names, all voices, Slip-Shape, this is Proteus, whoever that is, the shepherd of the seals, driving my many selves from cave to cave . . ."

This method is not about anthropomorphizing nature but rather engaging with it on its own terms, understanding its inherent rhythms, and unraveling its mysteries through language. Donna Haraway's concept of "staying with the trouble" and her advocacy for "making kin" with nonhuman entities provide a compelling lens to understand Oswald's approach.[5] Both Oswald and Haraway resist reductive dualisms that place humans at the center, aiming to foster more responsible, multi-species collaborations. Oswald's verses, in their attunement to the nonhuman, can be seen as practicing Haraway's plea for a more sympoietic (collaboratively "making-with") form of engagement with the world. McLean again:

> "If we accept that human lives and projects are inextricably intertwined with a host of other-than-human powers and presences (animal, vegetable, mineral, meteorological, etc.), how might we begin engage these in ways that do not reduce them to human-centered systems of explanation? Perhaps this demands a creative as much as an analytical or descriptive approach."

Stuart McLean studied literature before turning toward anthropology. In his anthropological pursuits, he often delved into the transformative potential of storytelling and fabulating.[6] McLean's approach celebrates narratives not as mere reflections of the world but as generative entities

[5] Donna J. Haraway, Staying With the Trouble: Making Kin in the Chthulucene (Durham: Duke University Press, 2016).
[6] Stuart McLean, Fictionalizing Anthropology: Encounters and Fabulations at the Edges of the Human (Minneapolis: University of Minnesota Press, 2017).

that shape and re-shape realities. Similarly, Oswald's poetic method, in its own right, can be considered a generative force. It not only narrates the nonhuman but also allows it to emerge, to affect and to be affected, enacting a poetic ecology that echoes McLean's understanding of stories. Alice Oswald's poetic engagements with the more-than-human resonate deeply with Haraway's conceptual frameworks and McLean's storytelling ethos. Together, they challenge anthropocentrism, urging us to reimagine our narratives and relationships with the vast web of life. In an era marked by environmental crises and a desperate need for cross-species understanding, their convergences might just point the way toward more ethical, imaginative, and interconnected futures.

Other anthropologists have explored the power of writing to build bridges with other states and dimensions of the world. The mentor and once dissertation supervisor of Stuart McLean, Michael Taussig, wrote a strange book blending reflections on sketching, as a mode of seeing and knowing, with a more general introspection on the act of taking field notes and writing them up —in *I Swear I Saw This: Drawings in Fieldwork Notebooks, Namely My Own*, Taussig also sends us to the radical experiments of the beat poets.[7] His approach to fieldwork and his emphasis on the interplay between reality and imagination is inspired, among many others sources, by the writer William S. Burroughs' own experimental narrative techniques. Both scholars and artists are concerned with how reality is represented, constructed, and understood, and the relations that can

---

[7] Swear I Saw This - Drawings in Fieldwork Notebooks, Namely My Own (Chicago ; London: University of Chicago Press, 2011).

be weaved with other realms through these practices.

During the workshop led by Stuart McLean, these approaches were explored in two ways: first with the reactivation of fieldwork fragments, as a collective bout of "writing up"; and then again with the practice of slashing the prose into free verse to feel the liveliness of written words: "cutting up". The "cut-up" method is a literary technique popularized by Burroughs in the late 1950s and 1960.[8] The method involves taking a linear text (or multiple texts) and physically cutting it into pieces, then rearranging those pieces to create a new text. The resultant work often has a disjointed, nonlinear, and sometimes surreal quality, as unexpected juxtapositions emerge from the rearranged text fragments. The origins of the "cut-up" method can be traced back to Dadaists like Tristan Tzara, but it was Brion Gysin, a painter and friend of Burroughs, who introduced the technique to him during their time together in Paris. Gysin reportedly came upon the method accidentally while cutting out newspaper clippings[9] In the exploration of anthropological narrative techniques, the "cut-up" method can be a key to unlocking multi-dimensional understandings. When juxtaposed with Alice Oswald's poetic engagement with the more-than-human, fascinating palimpsests emerge that challenges traditional anthropological narratives and push for a more intertwined human-nonhuman discourse. McLean likes to speak about the "edge-of-the-human": where we come close to the undefined and raw force of language beyond the agency of a (human) subject.

[8] see for an overview of Burroughs experimental methods Davis Schneiderman and Philip Walsh, eds., *Retaking The Universe: William S. Burroughs in the Age of Globalization*, First Edition (London ; Sterling, Va: Pluto Press, 2004).
[9] Marcus Boon, "The Book of Methods: Selected Writings on the Cut Up by William S. Burroughs and Brion Gysin," January 24, 2020, https://marcusboon.com/the-book-of-methods-selected-writings-on-the-cut-up-by-william-s-burroughs-and-brion-gysin/.

The "cut-up" technique collapses the boundaries between disparate textual and visual elements. Both methods challenge anthropocentrism in the creative writing process: Oswald, through her lyrical symbiosis with nature, and Burroughs, through the anarchic reconfiguration of language. Taussig's fieldwork, especially as articulated in *I Swear I Saw This*, exemplifies an anthropological cut-up. By incorporating drawings and nonlinear observations, he captures the dynamism of raw experience in ways traditional ethnographic methods most often miss. This could be compared to Oswald's effort to articulate the dynamic essence of the nonhuman, not through description but through embodied rhythm and sound. Drawing from the above, we can frame an emerging form of anthropological writing in Stuart McLean's practice that borrows from Oswald's poetics, Burroughs' cut-up, and Taussig's fieldwork aesthetics. It's a form that is more attuned to the rhythms of the world, more open to unexpected connections, and more inclusive of diverse voices. Just as Donna Haraway champions multi-species collaborations and generative storytelling, this anthropological perspective seeks to understand the world in its rich, complex, and ever-evolving tapestry.

The online version of this book presents the written pieces along with intertwined with "cuts" of the footage of Stuart's material, making use of the possibilities offered by digital publication to include the fragmentary format of the gif anime.[10] Working through a free associative process, editing this little collection felt like delivering a multimodal remix of Stuart's fieldwork. Thus, whether it's through poetic

[10] Pubpub originated from the idea of making it possible to insert gif anime into academic papers, cf. Jefferson Pooley, „The Case for PubPub", 3. August 2022, https://doi.org/10.5281/zenodo.6951450.

engagement, the radical open access publishing process, or fieldwork that blurs the lines between observer, the second order observer and the observed, a new frontier in anthropological writing beckons—one that makes space for stretching our senses, for the multifaceted ways of relate to the presences that populate our intertwined existences.

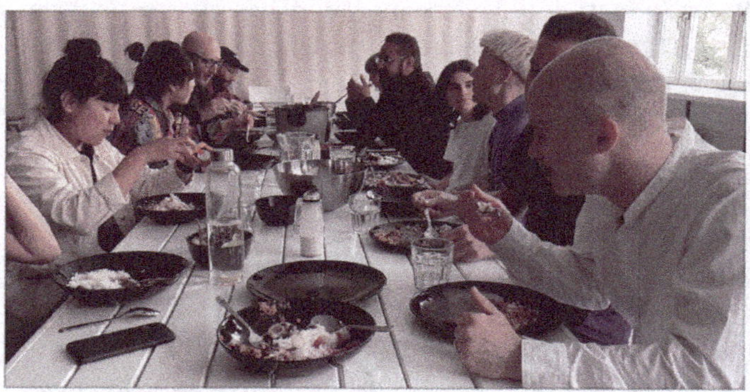

Workshop lunchtime @ Maxime Le Calvé, 11 May 2023

Flicker
A festival of impermanence
Stuart McLean

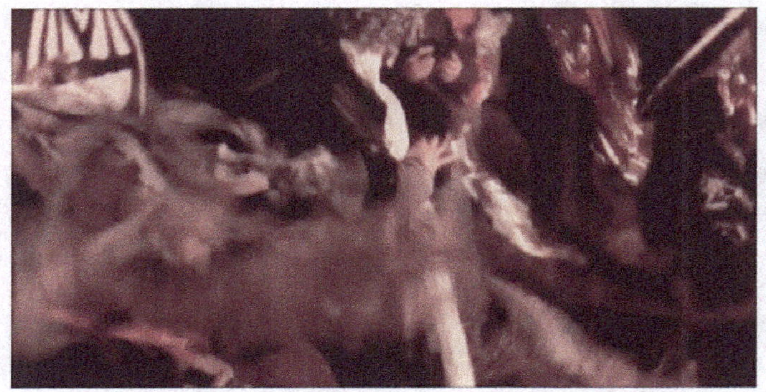

A festival of impermanence
of all that is not
monumental

it's comings and goings
microcosming
the pushy changefulness
of island weather

the wind is a character in this story
 unseen but very much present
tangibly so even

I take the early afternoon flight from Mainland, with two
of the artists - Gustav and Signe from Sweden, along with a
few islanders returning home with shopping bags

the wind holds and rocks the plane
as it rises, banks, and descends

toward the narrow airstrip
reminding you that air
is substance
stuff

no forgetting of air in Orkney!

then at night it sends showers of sparks streaming
horizontally from the torches
re-watching video footage of the bonfire, the flames seem to
be straining to escape
to the right of the frame, the direction of the wind

the wind is continuous sound
rhythmically rustling the fabrics of the costumes
unceasing and everywhere
yet also
irregular and
inconstant
gusting

the action is happening in the wind

"Fire action!" shouts Frog King

but the wind is already playing with the fire

stretching   and   elongating
it

d i s p e r s I n g
and
                        scattering
                        it

everything
is
flicker

faces and forms
glimpsed, then
disappeared

people are mostly standing still
but everything is motion
costumed bodies
mask-mutated faces
linking and dispersing
in a dapple-dance
of flame and darkness

mistaken-for-solid shapes
of daylit habit
undoing themselves
as though in homage
to whence they came

and still
the wind

the inconstancy
everywhere the same
and different
that is
the only
constant

a festival
of flicker

A Froggy Vision
I never got the chance to
see and touch is floating in
the wind. Caught in the gust.
Theodore Stanley

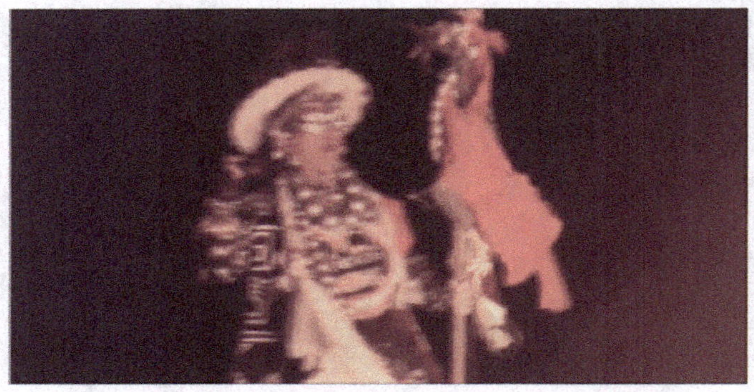

It's 1920. Grandpa Philip is only a wee lad. The full head of
hair
I never got the chance to see and touch is floating
in the wind.
Caught in the gust.

The war ended recently. History is propelling onwards
at an alarming rate. But here time stood still.
Do wind and time hurtle on in an inverse relation?
Is it still in Moscow? Wind free in Berlin? Calm in Koln?

Sun sets. Frog appears. Ribbet ribbet.
Frog seems out of place. Black and grey and silver and gold
are striking in this wash of blue and green.
Frog takes out his camera and walks towards Grandpa
Philip.

Framing his face and billowing hair in the sightfinder.
Keeping Philip in the centre of his vision, Frog continues,
face still.

Why is Frog holding the camera?
Is the camera from Hong Kong?
What would my grandfather say if he saw Frog from Hong
Kong holding a camera
to fend off the wind that blows out our fire?
Would he see a vision of the future not yet come or a past
still oncoming?

Cardboard Hat
Who tells the untold stories of survivals?
Wendy Chua

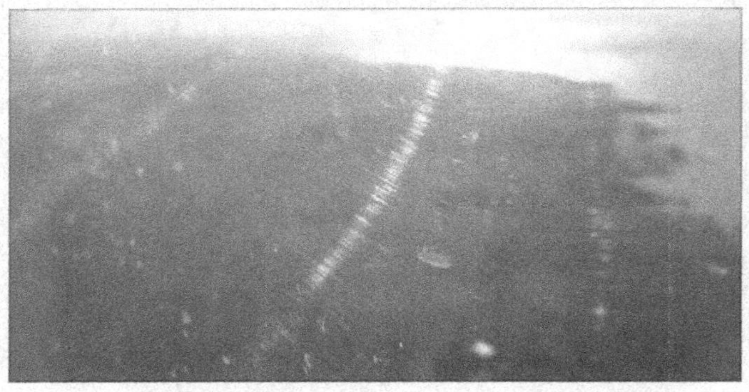

Trembling titanium, slowly descending,

tak tak tak tak tak tak …

pulling up at the island of the nomads,

the evicted, the deserted and the left-behinds,

the stateless and the rootless diaspora.

The spirit beckons, fires up the totem,

pouring fuel and pungent rubber fumes.

The enchanted watches, spellbound,

writing myths and reseeding souls through rituals.

Resurrecting through burning;

who tells the untold stories of survivals?

Whispered through frog eyes and a cardboard hat,
Where is my net? My bag? My sling and my sack?

Burning Purpose No More

A small world, grazing on the sea.
Maxime Le Calvé

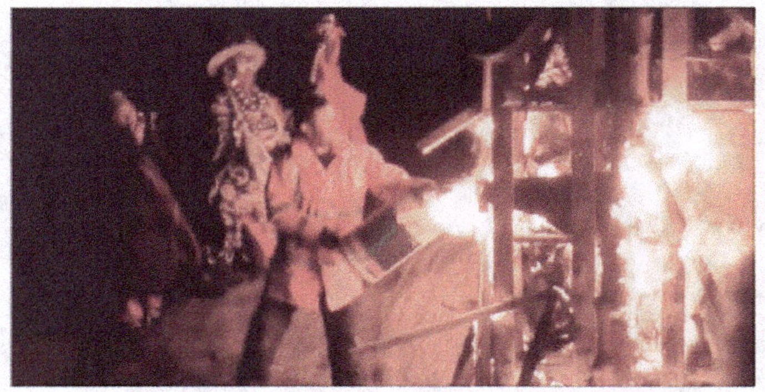

The island is a world standing,

laying low,

prostrated,

grazing on the sea, by itself.

What is grazing there on the island,

what is happening there in the houses,

What is taking shape in the sandy soil and the avian
reserve,

       this is all island life.

Not a shortcoming

of what is happening on the continent,

but a world by itself. Intertwined with other worlds,
and other happenings.

The islanders are screaming "fire,

     fire" and the wind is invited to propagate

the burning of material amassed here

    on the beach and in the garages,

throughout the year.

Pieces of crates bringing goods to the island,

Of trees tossed across the channel,

  bits

              and pieces

       of houses that crumbled away,

  tired tires good for the fire

and nothing else, no more.

The island is a small world breeding with the sea,

a piece of land barely offered

and rather captured

and seized

by a group of human grazers,

processing the grass of the island through the
domesticated sheep.

The great grass beings

and their fungi siblings

are turning rock wind and sun

into

sparse

stuff.

Praise the blade of grass.

A firefighter is throwing gasoline

on the fire.

With a focussed face, without showing much of his

yet obvious

joy,

He is nurturing his purpose in one divergent instance.

The festival is an inversion.

The fireman knows

what he is doing.

The purpose fire

animates   the spirit

all what's in between, no more.

           Flammable stuff

stitching

a body of heat and light

in the plentiful air, the breath from the sea monsters,

the saga warriors and the foam of the waves

splashing in darkness with

                              almost

no one to hear them.

잇는것 The thing that connect

If tales and sensations
enshroud the isle, then
.reality lies therein
Yoonha Kim

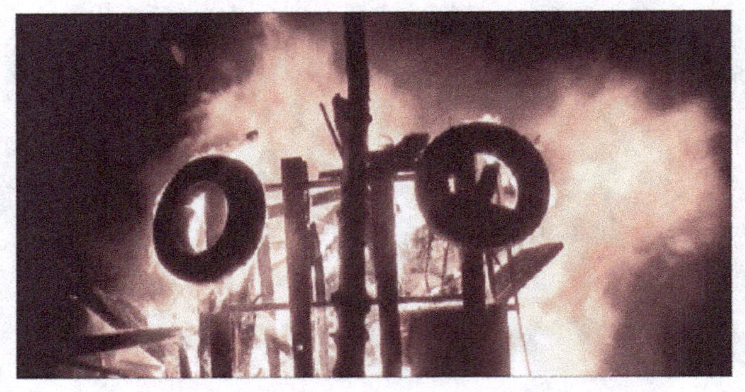

.긴가민가한 기억이 있다

꼭 일어난 것만 같은데 상상이 반인 것도 같
은

그때 솨아솨아한 빠른 바람 소리, 딱딱한 기
체가 철컹거리는 소리와 타닥이는 장작의 온
기가 부재한 기억에 확신을 준다

그 섬에 나는 없었다

꿔온 촉감과 귀를 따갑게 하는 것들은 있었
다

있는 것은 잇는 것이다

섬을 둘러싼 이야기들과 느낌으로 이어진다
면 진짜 있는것은 그런 것들이다

In the penumbra of doubt lingers a memory,

Seemingly real as though it transpired, yet half is but
a dream,

The susurrus of a brisk zephyr, the unyielding clank of
metal,

And the warmth of crackling logs absent in memory,
endow certainty.

I was not upon that isle,

Yet borrowed tactility and sharp sounds did exist,

Existence(itt-da) is relating/connecting(it-da),

If tales and sensations enshroud the isle, then reality
lies therein.

One Hundred Souls
Across the blue. A trembling approximation, searching.
Sandro Simon

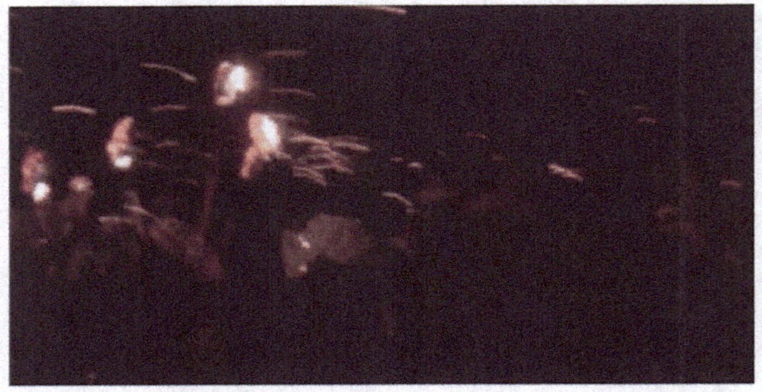

Across the blue. A trembling approximation,
searching

The image, blown off

The motor, roaring

The waves, roaring, underneath, inaudible.

Barrenness erupts from the blue.

Across the green. A panning approximation

The image, searching

Searching for its place, amongst

Dancers

Singers

A fireman making fire.

Petrol on wood, neither of which actually exist here.

The wind scatters every sprouting tree

eats into the bodies

piles up the waves.

The wind shreds the words

carries away the sparks

carries away the memories of the dead.

They burn holes into the night.

Embers Fly. Sparks Float.

Approached from the sky, the inhabitants' habitations sparsely populate the patchwork countryside, the neatly defined, if unproductive fields.
Geoffrey Garrison

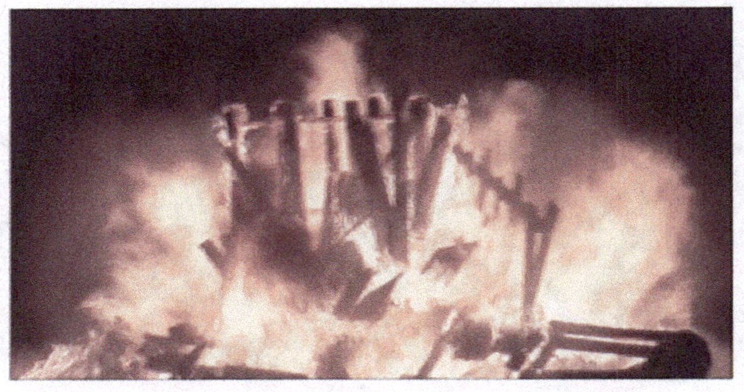

Approached from the sky, the inhabitants' habitations

sparsely populate the patchwork countryside,

the neatly defined, if unproductive fields.

And I wonder if the harvest – potatoes? cabbage? –

livestock – mutton? lamb? – and catch – herring and
cod? –

will be plentiful enough to make it through the
winter,

the months when the ship cannot reach the island

to bring packaged, processed flavors and calories, and
other signs of so-called civilization.

From above we see the wind in the treeless landscape.

At night we set alight

an effigy of what we would like our past to have been

(we, I say, an imagined community of artists, visitors,
locals,

the odd atavistic goatherd,

and the lone, pyromaniacal fireman).

But we're not alone here; the ghosts of our CO_2
footprint have traveled with us

across the seas, the skies, the roads,
and all that we know and have seen and have heard
before.

Embers fly.

Sparks float.

Inferno

Archipelago

Notes and Drawings
A workshop documentation.
by Geoffrey Garrison

He's looking at the other-than-human in human creativity, in human artefacts.

Art festival in Orkney archipelago

Papay Gyro Nights

Tiny, treeless island transformed into an arts space based on mythical figure, grantees incorporating other-than-human aspects

11 May 2023

"Encounters and Fabulations" at
the Edges of the Human"

Writing Workshop hosted by
Maxime Le Calvé

Rock art at   Kimberley, Western
                            Australia

                continually retouched
                — no author

"They made themselves"

Lucretius = epic
poem treatise on physics

Michel Serres book on Lucretius

Michel Serres' Eyebrows!

Stuart is aiming to think beyond nature/culture dichotomy — specifically vis-à-vis human creativity

Karen Barad, Vinciane Despret, indigenous thinkers, all things we've been looking at, at SOE recently — Marisol d.l.C., Philippe Descola, Emanuele Coccia, Eduardo Kohn, …

Edward Burnett Tylor talked
about "survivals" — traditions
that continue to be practiced whose
origins had been lost, or the significance
was no longer clear
influenced Aby Warburg's idea
of 'Nachleben'

And
Georges
Didi-Huberman

— Problematizing past
vs. now

Survivals as in-the-present
but not necessarily of-the-
present

animism as survival
Survivals as lessons for the future

Simon O'Sullivan, artist & media
scholar

Fréger's photographs
of survivals (Erbsenbären, etc.)

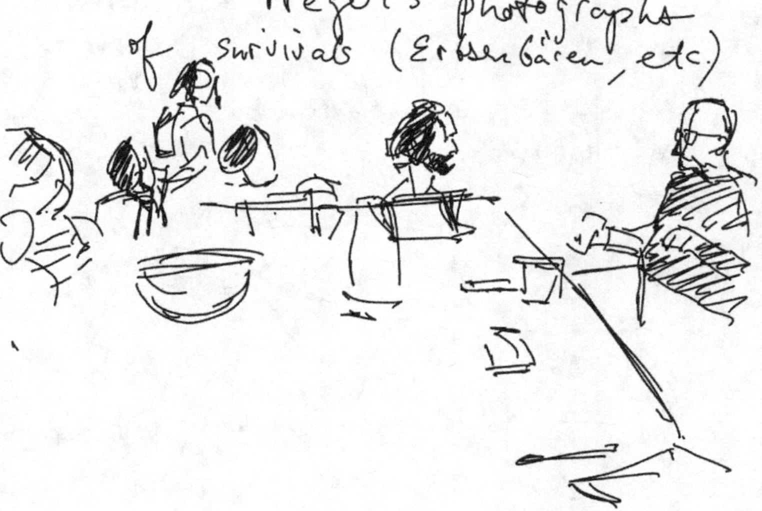

www.ingramcontent.com/pod-product-compliance
Lightning Source LLC
Chambersburg PA
CBHW051847250726
48659CB00006B/2075